J

W9-AJP-826

Oft

Spiders

and Other Arachnids

Concept and Product Development: Editorial Options, Inc.
Series Designer: Karen Donica
Book Author: Steven Otfinoski

**For information on other World Book
products, visit us at our Web site at
http://www.worldbook.com**

**For information on sales to schools and libraries
in the United States, call 1-800-975-3250.**

**For information on sales to schools and libraries
in Canada, call 1-800-837-5365.**

World Book, Inc.
233 N. Michigan Avenue
Chicago, IL 60601

Library of Congress Cataloging-in-Publication Data

Spiders and other arachnids.
     p. cm. -- (World Book's animals of the world)
  ISBN 0-7166-1220-8 -- ISBN 0-7166-1211-9 (set)
   1. Spiders--Juvenile literature. 2. Arachnida--Juvenile literature. [1. Spiders.
2. Arachnids.] I. World Book, Inc. II. Series.

  QL458.4 S645 2001
  595.4'4--dc21   2001017529

Printed in Singapore
1 2 3 4 5 6 7 8 9 05 04 03 02 01

World Book's Animals of the World

Spiders
and Other Arachnids

Why would I fail
an eye test?

World Book, Inc.
A Scott Fetzer Company
Chicago

Contents

Why "might" I inspire spring cleaning?

How do I have a
web address?

Why does my tail
mean the end for
others?

What Is an Arachnid?

An arachnid *(uh RAK nihd)* is a small, insectlike animal that lives mostly on land. The animal you see here is an arachnid. It's not an insect—even though it may look like one. Can you name it? Yes, it's a spider.

The word *arachnid* comes from a Greek myth about a weaver. In this story, a girl named Arachne *(uh RAK nee)* boasts that she can weave better than Athena, the goddess of arts and crafts. Arachne even challenges Athena to a contest! When Athena sees how well Arachne weaves, she, the goddess, becomes angry. She rips Arachne's fabric. Then she turns Arachne into a spider to spin and weave through all time.

Spiders are the only arachnids that spin and weave silk. But spiders are not the only arachnids. Other arachnids include scorpions, ticks, mites, and harvestmen, which are also known as daddy longlegs.

Black and yellow spider

Where in the World Do Arachnids Live?

Arachnids live nearly everywhere on Earth. They live in grassy fields and wet swamps. They live in hot, sandy deserts and in cool, dark caves. They live in tropical rain forests and on rocky mountaintops. In fact, arachnids live anywhere they can find food.

One arachnid you have probably seen is a spider. So far, scientists have found more than 30,000 kinds of spiders. And scientists think there are many, many more to be discovered.

These pictures show some places where you can see arachnids. But if you really want to see a spider, you don't have to look very far. There is probably a spider not too far from you right now.

Swamp

Desert

Cave

Rain forest

Is It a Spider or an Insect?

You see a small creature scurry across the floor. But you aren't sure if it is a spider or an insect. How do you decide? Do what scientists do. First, they take a close look at the animal. They count its legs. They count its body parts, too. These are the best clues to use when deciding if a creature is a spider or an insect.

Look at the drawings as a scientist might. Count the legs. Did you count six legs, three on each side? Good. An insect has six legs. Did you count eight legs on the spider? That's right. A spider has eight legs, not six. If you count the body parts, you see another difference. An insect has three main body parts. A spider has only two main body parts.

Legs and body parts are just two ways in which insects and spiders are different. Take a closer look at the drawings. What other differences do you see?

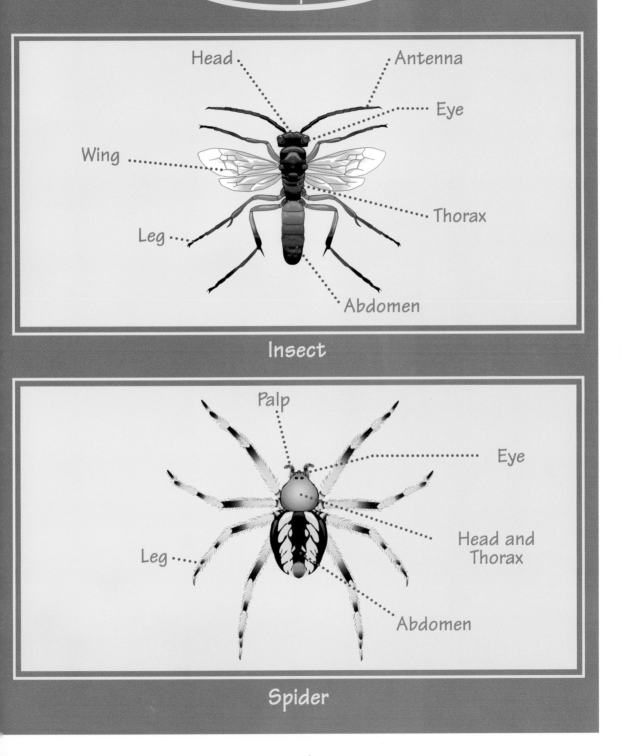

Diagrams of Insect and Spider

Insect

- Head
- Antenna
- Eye
- Wing
- Thorax
- Leg
- Abdomen

Spider

- Palp
- Eye
- Head and Thorax
- Leg
- Abdomen

What Do Spiders Look Like?

Spiders come in different shapes and sizes. They come in different colors, too. But all spiders have things in common. Look at this spider. Like all spiders, it has two main body parts and eight legs. Now look at the spider's head. What do you see?

Notice the spider's eyes. Most spiders, including this one, have eight eyes. Yet most spiders don't see very well. They depend on the hairs on their legs and their short, leglike palps to help them sense things. The hairs help spiders to hear, feel, and smell.

Spiders have no bones. A spider's soft body is protected by a hard, outside shell. This shell is called an exoskeleton *(EHK soh SKEHL uh tuhn).* It fits over the spider's soft body like a suit of armor. As a spider grows, it grows a new exoskeleton and sheds its old one. This is called molting.

Arrow-shaped spider

How Does a Spider Kill Its Prey?

Most spiders eat insects and other spiders. A few large spiders eat frogs, birds, or small lizards. But all spiders kill their prey with a poisonous bite. A spider bites its prey with its fangs, which are long, pointed teeth. Poison, called venom *(VEHN uhm),* flows through the fangs. The venom stuns or kills the spider's prey.

Now the spider has a problem. It has no chewing parts in its mouth. It cannot eat its prey by chewing. Instead, the spider sucks the liquids from its prey. A spider may also spray special juices from its mouth onto the prey. These juices turn the prey's body into a soupy liquid. Then the spider can slurp up its meal.

But what if the spider isn't hungry? A spider simply stuns its prey. Then it spins and weaves a silk case around the prey. The spider hangs the prey on its web or puts it in a safe place. When the spider does get hungry, it has a meal waiting.

Jumping spider
with prey

How Do Spiders Make Silk?

All spiders have special silk glands that make silk. This silk comes out through tiny, fingerlike tubes called spinnerets *(SPIHN uh rehts)*. The spinnerets spin the silk into different kinds of thread.

A spider may have as many as six silk glands. Each gland makes a different kind of silk. Some silk is sticky and some isn't. Spiders can combine the silk to make many different kinds of threads.

One kind of thread is called a dragline. Spiders use draglines in many ways. A spider may use its dragline to drop down from a high place and to climb back up again. A female spider may use her dragline as a trail. A male spider may follow this trail when it is looking for a mate. Draglines also help spiders catch prey and escape from danger.

Spider silk is an amazing material. It is waterproof. And it is very strong. In fact, it is the strongest natural fiber on Earth.

Spinnerets

Why Do Spiders Spin Webs?

Spiders spin many kinds of webs. But all webs are used for the same thing—to capture prey.

The threads in a spider web are thin and hard to see. If an insect comes along, it may not see the web until it is too late. Its legs and body get stuck on the sticky strands of silk. The more the insect struggles, the more trapped it becomes.

Some spiders sit and wait in the middle of their webs. The spider may not see a trapped insect. But the spider can feel it tug and pull on the web. The spider knows that dinner has arrived!

Other spiders sit on the edge of their webs. When they feel tugs, they use draglines to swing down onto their prey.

Garden spider with prey

Which Spiders Spin the Prettiest Webs?

Many people think that orb weavers, like this garden spider, spin the prettiest webs. These webs are especially beautiful when they are wet with morning dew or covered with frost.

Orb webs are large and round. The main threads look like the spokes on a bicycle wheel. These threads are made up of dry silk. Threads of loose, sticky silk connect the spokes. The sticky threads are the ones that trap the spider's prey.

Why doesn't a spider get caught in its own web? There are two reasons. First, a spider knows where the sticky threads are in its own web. It can avoid these threads. Second, spiders have special claws on their feet. The claws keep a spider from losing its grip and falling onto the sticky strands.

Orb weavers are fussy builders. A spider may tear down its web each night and build a new one. It may even eat the old web to recycle the silk.

Garden spider

What Shapes Can Webs Have?

Some spiders spin tangled webs with threads that go every which way. Others spin sheet webs that hang like hammocks between leaves and branches. Still others spin funnel webs.

A funnel web is shaped like a funnel—wide at one end and narrow at the other. The funnel-web spider hides in the narrow end. It waits for an insect to fly or to crawl into the wide end of the web. As the prey struggles to free itself, the spider runs out and kills it.

Funnel-web spiders are sometimes called grass spiders. This is because they usually build their webs in the grass or along the ground.

22

Funnel-web spider

How Did Black Widows Get Their Name?

Female black widows sometimes kill and eat their mates. With their mates dead, the spiders are now "widows." And that's how black widows got their name.

A female black widow doesn't always eat her mate. But like most web weavers, her vision is poor. She sometimes mistakes her tiny mate—who is only about one-fourth her size—for a tasty meal.

Most female black widows weave tangled webs in dark places. They build webs under fallen logs or in the corners of barns and sheds. If you see a black widow, don't touch it. Its bite is harmful to humans. It can cause illness and even death. Fortunately, the spider bites only as a last defense.

You can recognize a female black widow by the red or yellow hourglass shape on its abdomen. With its legs stretched out, a female is about 1 1/2 inches (3.8 centimeters) long.

Female and male
black widows

Why Do Spiders Spin Silk Sacs?

Spiders spin webs to capture prey. They wrap their prey in silk. They spin nests to live in. But most female spiders also spin silk sacs to hold their eggs.

The number of eggs a female lays depends on her size. An average-sized female lays about 100 eggs at a time. A large spider may lay as many as 2,000 eggs at one time.

After laying her eggs, a female spider wraps them in a silk cocoon called an egg sac. Then she puts the egg sac in a safe place. Some spiders hang their egg sacs in their webs. Others attach them to leaves or plants. Still others, like this wolf spider, carry their egg sacs with them.

Spiderlings, or baby spiders, hatch inside the egg sac. But they don't come out right away. They need to be able to spin their own silk before they can leave the safety of the sac.

Wolf spider with egg sac

How Do Spiderlings Travel?

Spiderlings travel in a special way. It is called ballooning. First, a spiderling climbs to the top of a plant or other tall object. Then it tilts its spinnerets up into the air. The moving air pulls silk threads from the spinnerets. The threads act like a balloon and lift the tiny spider into the air.

Ballooning spiderlings can travel long distances. Sailors have even seen ballooning spiderlings more than 200 miles (320 kilometers) from land!

But ballooning has its problems. The spiderlings must travel wherever the wind takes them. Some spiderlings are lucky. They land in new places to begin new lives. Others are not so lucky. They land in the water and drown, or they are eaten by predators.

Spiderlings

When Is a Wolf Spider Gentle As a Lamb?

A wolf spider has silk glands, but it doesn't spin a web. A wolf spider is a hunting spider. Like most hunting spiders, it has good vision. It runs after and pounces on its prey. The wolf spider leaps into the air to catch a flying insect. But this fierce hunter is a very gentle parent.

A female wolf spider attaches her egg sac to her spinnerets and carries it with her. She guards the egg sac. She inspects it and repairs it. When the eggs are ready to hatch, she breaks open the sac so that the spiderlings can get out.

The spiderlings travel on their mother's back. They hang on tightly to hairs there. If a spiderling falls off, it follows its mother's dragline to find her. Then it quickly climbs up one of her legs. Now that's a leg to stand on!

Wolf spider with spiderlings

Which Spider Nets Its Prey?

Some spiders use silk to trap prey in unusual ways. A good example is the ogre-faced stick spider. This spider uses a silk net.

During the day, an ogre-faced stick spider doesn't move. It is so motionless that it looks like a broken twig. But at night, the spider is busy. It spins a tiny web, no bigger than a postage stamp. It holds the web in its front legs and waits. When an insect passes by, the spider quickly stretches out the net to several times its size. Then it throws the net over the insect.

Ogre-faced stick spiders catch insects in the air and on the ground. As an insect flies by, its wings give off vibrations. The ogre-faced stick spider senses these vibrations and lunges its net at the insect. The spider uses its eyes to find prey that is moving on the ground.

Ogre-faced
stick spider

Which Spider Is the Largest?

There are many different kinds of tarantulas *(tuh RAN chuh luhz)*. The spider in this picture is a Goliath *(guh LY uhth)* bird tarantula. It is feeding on a bird that fell from its nest. This tarantula is the largest spider in the world. Including its legs, it can measure 10 inches (25 centimeters) across!

Some tropical tarantulas live in trees. These tarantulas are also called bird spiders. Most tarantulas, however, live in underground burrows.

Unlike most hunting spiders, a tarantula has poor vision. To find prey, it may spin triplines near its burrow. When an insect walks over a tripline, the tarantula runs along the line and captures the prey. Sometimes, a tarantula will take prey as big as a frog or a small lizard.

Tarantulas look fierce, but most have bites that are harmless to people. In fact, some people even keep tarantulas as pets!

Goliath bird tarantula

How Does the Trap-Door Spider Catch Its Prey?

Trap-door spiders are tarantulas. Each trap-door spider makes an underground burrow lined with silk. At the entrance to its burrow, this spider builds a trap door. Like the spider in the picture, it waits behind the door for its next meal to pass by. Then it throws open its trap door, rushes out, and grabs the prey. The spider poisons the prey and drags it into its burrow.

Most trap-door spiders disguise their trap doors. They weave bits of mud, sand, and other materials into the trap doors. In this way, a spider's trap door looks like the ground around it. Insects don't notice the trap until it is too late.

Trap-door spider

How Do Crab Spiders Use Camouflage?

Crab spiders don't spin webs or build traps. They are sit-and-wait hunters. They sit on flowers and wait for insects to arrive. Why don't insects notice them? Crab spiders can camouflage *(KAM puh flahzh),* or hide, their bodies. Some change color to match the color of the flowers they sit on.

Crab spiders blend into their surroundings in other ways, too. Some have white and gray spots on their bodies. They pull their legs in and sit on leaves or plants. These spiders look like bird droppings!

Crab spiders are small. Most are no bigger than flies. Yet a crab spider can kill an insect much larger than itself. When a crab spider is finished sucking the liquids from its prey, all that is left is the prey's exoskeleton.

Crab spider
on goldenrod

How Far Can a Jumping Spider Jump?

Believe it or not, some jumping spiders can jump 40 times the length of their bodies. That's a jumper!

Jumping spiders don't jump for exercise. They jump to capture prey. And jumping spiders don't wait for prey, as most hunting spiders do. Jumping spiders have the best eyesight in the spider world. They use their vision to stalk, or follow, prey. Then they pounce!

This picture shows how a spider anchors its dragline to a surface, leaps into the air, and prepares to land on its prey. Can you see its dragline? When the spider lands on its prey, it sinks in its fangs and holds on.

Jumping spider

Can Water Spiders Breathe Underwater?

In a way, water spiders can breathe underwater. Water spiders live in underwater webs shaped like small bells. Each bell has an opening. A water spider carries air bubbles from the surface of the water and takes them into its bell. The bubbles slowly push all the water out of the bell, leaving the air trapped inside. A water spider can live on the air in its "diving bell" for several months.

Inside its bell, a water spider waits for a water bug to swim by or for a flying insect to fall into the water. Then the spider swims to grab its prey and bring it back to its underwater home.

Water spiders are the only spiders that live most of their lives underwater. These special spiders live in the lakes and ponds of Europe and in parts of Asia.

Water spider in
underwater web

What Looks Like a Spider but Isn't?

The spiderlike animals you see in the picture are called harvestmen. You may also know them by their nickname—daddy longlegs. These arachnids look like spiders, but they aren't spiders. In fact, they are different from spiders in many ways.

Unlike spiders, harvestmen do not spin silk. And they do not have venom glands or fangs. If you look closely, you also see that a harvestman's body seems to have only one large body part. That's because a harvestman doesn't have a tiny "spider" waist.

Harvestmen have tiny mouthparts that allow them to grind up their food. They eat insects and plants. Harvestmen do not bite, so they are harmless to people. Some can, however, give off a bad odor if they are disturbed.

Harvestmen

How Are Scorpions Like Spiders?

Like spiders, scorpions *(SKAWR pee uhnz)* are arachnids. They have two main body parts and eight legs. And like spiders, scorpions have hairs, called bristles, along their legs. These bristles feel vibrations on the ground. They tell the scorpion, which has poor vision, when prey is near.

Most scorpions are larger than spiders. Their body parts are larger, too. Look at the scorpion's head. Instead of spider fangs, a scorpion has pincers that grab and tear prey. Instead of leglike palps, a scorpion has a large set of claws that hold and crush prey.

Now look at the scorpion's body. The last few segments of the scorpion's abdomen form a long "tail." Do you know how a scorpion uses its tail? Read on to find out.

Scorpion

Why Is a Scorpion's Tail So Dangerous?

A scorpion often kills its prey with venom. But a scorpion doesn't use fangs to deliver its poison. It uses the stinger at the end of its tail. First, the scorpion grabs its prey with its claws. Then it raises its tail up and over its head to sting its prey.

The sting of a scorpion is very powerful. It kills insects and spiders instantly. And it can be deadly to larger animals. Still, many animals—such as lizards, snakes, owls, and mammals—feed on scorpions.

Scorpions are nocturnal animals. They hunt and feed mostly at night. During the day, scorpions hide among rocks, in cracks on the ground, and under the bark of trees. A scorpion's sting can be painful, but most scorpions are not dangerous to humans.

Sahara yellow scorpion

How Do Scorpions Care for Their Young?

All female scorpions give birth to live young. And they take care of their young for a short time, too. A female scorpion carries her young on her back until they are ready to live on their own.

A female scorpion gives birth to a litter, or a group, of about 25 baby scorpions. Each scorpion is born with a thin layer of tissue around its body. With its mother's help, the newborn breaks out of this thin sack. Then it crawls onto its mother's back.

Newborn scorpions are pale in color. In the first few days of their lives, they are totally defenseless. They depend on their mothers for protection. Young scorpions stay with their mothers a week or more, until their first molt.

Scorpion with young

How Did the Whip Scorpion Get Its Name?

One look at a whip scorpion helps you decide how this animal got its name. It looks like a scorpion with a whip for a tail. But this arachnid is not a true scorpion. Its tail has no stinger.

Whip scorpions hunt for insects and other prey at night. Whip scorpions use their front claws as feelers to help them find their way. When a whip scorpion locates an insect, it uses its claws to grab and crush its prey.

A whip scorpion doesn't have a sting to defend itself, but it does have strong claws. And those claws deliver a painful pinch! Some whip scorpions have another defense. These scorpions spray a mist from their tails. The mist is made of a vinegarlike acid that can hurt and burn an enemy.

Whip scorpion

Which Arachnids Are the Smallest?

Mites are the smallest arachnids. In fact, many mites are as small as, or smaller than, the period at the end of this sentence. They can be seen clearly only under a microscope. The mite shown here has been greatly magnified so that you can see it. Also, color has been added.

Some mites are parasites *(PAHR uh SYTS),* or animals that live and feed on other animals. Many of these mites burrow under the skin and cause itchy rashes. Others feed on the blood of animals. Mites that live this way often spread diseases. Still other mites destroy food products, such as grain or cheese.

One kind of mite even likes dust! Dust mites prefer warm, dusty places—such as under a bed or in a carpet. These mites are so small that people don't notice them. But when you see a dust mite magnified, you'll want to clean your room! Dust mites don't bite. But their body wastes can cause allergies and asthma.

Dust mite

Which "Spider" Is Really a Mite?

Don't let the red spider's name confuse you. The red spider is really a mite. It just looks like a spider. And it is not always red. Red spider mites may also be green, yellow, or orange.

The red spider mite feeds on plants, which it sometimes destroys. The mite uses its sharp mouthparts to rip open leaf cells. This damages the leaves—and may cause the plant to die.

A red spider is about the size of a grain of salt. Because the mite is so small, it is often detected by the damage it causes.

European red
spider mite

What Is a Tick?

A tick is an arachnid. It is similar to a mite, only larger. In fact, you don't need a magnifying glass to see most ticks.

All ticks are parasites. They feed on the blood of other animals. Most live in fields and woods. Ticks lie among fallen leaves or on plants that grow low to the ground. If an animal brushes against the plant, the tick will leap onto its body. The tick begins to suck the host's blood until its own body blows up like a tiny balloon. Then the tick falls off and molts. It waits for a new host to pass by so it can have another meal.

Most ticks are harmless to animals and humans. But some spread diseases, such as Rocky Mountain spotted fever, Lyme disease, and relapsing fever.

Deer tick

Are Arachnids in Danger?

As a group, arachnids are not in danger. Still, some arachnids are in trouble. Let's look at two examples.

Many people wanted Mexican redknee tarantulas as pets. So many of these spiders were collected from the wild that they became threatened, or reduced in number. Today, laws protect these and other wild spiders that could also make good pets. Now pet spiders come from special breeding farms.

Six kinds of cave spiders in Texas are endangered. Polluted water is seeping into the caves where the spiders live. People are working to keep the caves clean. But these spiders face another danger. Fire ants have moved into their habitats. Fire ants not only eat the spiders' food, but they also eat the spiders themselves!

Yes, some spiders are in danger. But many, many more are not. As they have done for millions of years, spiders will continue to weave and spin.

Mexican redknee
tarantula

Arachnid Fun Facts

→ Most spiders live about a year. But some female tarantulas can live up to 20 years in captivity.

→ The bolas spider catches prey in an unusual way. It spins a silk "lasso" with a sticky silk ball at the end. It swings this thread to lasso and pull in its prey.

→ Some people have a fear of spiders. This fear is called arachnophobia *(uh RAK nih FOH bee uh)*.

→ In most animal groups, the males are larger than the females. But in the spider world, the females are larger than the males.

→ With some spider species, if a spider loses a leg, it will grow a new one the next time it molts.

Glossary

abdomen The back section of a spider's body.

arachnid A small animal without a backbone. It has two body parts and four pairs of legs.

ballooning A way in which spiderlings travel through the air on silk threads.

camouflage To change in appearance in order to hide.

dragline A silk line that spiders attach to objects as they move from one place to another.

egg sac A silk case that a female spider spins to hold her eggs.

endangered In danger of dying out.

exoskeleton A tough, outer body covering.

litter Young produced by an animal at one birth.

molt To lose fur, skin, or another body covering before getting a new one.

nocturnal Active at night.

palps Leglike parts on the sides of a spider's head.

parasite An animal that lives on or in another animal and feeds from it.

pincer A claw.

prey Any animal that is hunted for food by another animal.

silk A fine, strong fiber produced by spiders.

silk glands Small organs in a spider's body that produce liquid silk.

spiderling A baby spider.

spinnerets Fingerlike tubes on a spider's abdomen through which silk leaves the body.

thorax The second part of an insect's body, between the head and the abdomen.

tripline A silk line that spiders lay to sense the approach of an insect or other prey.

venom A poisonous liquid.

(**Boldface** indicates a photo, map, or illustration.)

Index

Picture Acknowledgments: Front & Back Cover: © Adam Jones, Photo Researchers; © Ken Brate, Photo Researchers; © Jane Burton, Bruce Coleman Collection; © David T. Roberts, Photo Researchers; © Jan Stromme, Bruce Coleman Inc.

© A. Cosmos Blank, Photo Researchers 37; © Ken Brate, Photo Researchers 39; © Jane Burton, Bruce Coleman Collection 43; © Gerald S. Cubitt, Bruce Coleman Collection 9; © Stephen Dalton, Photo Researchers 21; © Michael P. Fogden, Bruce Coleman Inc. 33; © Adam Jones, Photo Researchers 3, 7, 45; © Craig K. Lorenz, Photo Researchers 9; © Robert Lubeck, Animals Animals 9; © Oliver Meckes, Photo Researchers 4, 55; © John Mitchell, Photo Researchers 35; © Hans Pfletschinger, Peter Arnold Inc. 17; © Ivan Polunin, Bruce Coleman Inc. 29; © Andrew Purcell, Bruce Coleman Collection 9; © Gary Retherford, Photo Researchers 53; © David T. Roberts, Photo Researchers 23; © James H. Robinson, Photo Researchers 5, 13, 25; © Gregory K. Scott, Photo Researchers 31; © John Shaw, Bruce Coleman Collection 15; © Jan Stromme, Bruce Coleman Inc. 5, 47; © Karl H. Switak, Photo Researchers 51; © Kim Taylor, Bruce Coleman Collection 19, 27, 41; © Peter Ward, Bruce Coleman Inc. 49; © Larry West, Bruce Coleman Inc. 59; © Roy Whitehead, Photo Researchers 57; © Rod Williams, Bruce Coleman Collection 61.

Illustrations: WORLD BOOK illustration by Michael DiGiorgio 11; WORLD BOOK illustration by Karen Donica 62.

Arachnid Classification

Scientists classify animals by placing them into groups. The animal kingdom is a group that contains all the world's animals. Phylum, class, order, and family are smaller groups. Each phylum contains many classes. A class contains orders, and a family contains individual species. Each species also has its own scientific name. Here is how the animals in this book fit in to this system.

Arachnids and their relatives (Phylum Arthropoda)

Arachnids (Class Arachnida)

Harvestmen or daddy-long-legs (Order Opiliones)

Mites and Ticks (Order Acari)

Scorpions (Order Scorpiones)

Spiders and tarantulas (Order Araneae)

Black widows and their relatives (Family Theridiidae)

Black widow . . . . *Latrodectus mactans*

Crab spiders (Family Thomisidae)

Funnel web spiders and the water spider (Family Agelenidae)

Water spider . . . . *Argyroneta aquatica*

Jumping spiders (Family Salticidae)

Nursery web spiders (Family Pisauridae)

Ogre-faced stick spiders (Family Deinopidae)

Orb weavers (Family Araneidae)

Bolas spiders . . . . *Mastophora*
Yellow garden spider . . . . *Argiope aurantra*

Wolf spiders (Family Lycosidae)

Tarantulas (Family Theraphosidae)

Bird spider . . . . *Theraphosa blondi*
Red-kneed tarantula . . . . *Brachypelma smithi*

Trap-door spiders (Family Ctenizidae)

Whipscorpions (Order Uropygi)